# Lunch in Prague

## Authentic Meals from the Czech Republic

By: Layla Tacy

# License Notes

The content of this publication is protected by national and international copyright laws. Hence, you may not reproduce, edit, copy, print, or distribute any part of it, except with express permission of the author.

The author also reserves the right not to be liable for any inference, assumption, or misinterpretation which might lead to any form of damage.

# Table of Contents

# Introduction

We didn't know much about the Czech Republic when we first arrived here, but, to our surprise, most of their dishes are heavily meat-based with either beef, pork, or wild game. Many side dishes also use poultry as their main ingredient. Despite this, there is also an essential culture around fresh fruits and vegetables in the local cuisine. With lots of rural areas, a large part of the produce is grown there organically, meaning you can always count on the highest-quality ingredients for your meals.

And, while the cuisine is undoubtedly meat-based, it's the wide variety of fresh ingredients that make way for lots of delicious vegetarian meals too! Whatever your dietary requirements are, we're sure you can find something to your liking with our cookbook because we've made sure to include a wide variety of recipes for all types of food enthusiasts. We don't want you to skip out on any of the good stuff as we did for many years before flying to Prague a couple of months ago!

Now that we've tried the food, we're never letting it go! So much so that we've even prepared this cookbook for you. We've got wild rice soup, rye bread pudding, roast pork, cookies, couscous, meatloaf, and so much more. You've got Prague at your fingertips, so what's the excuse now? Let's get cooking! Good luck!

xxxxxxxxxxxxxxxxxxxxxxxxxxxxxxxxxxxxxxxxxxxxxxxxxxxxxxxx

# Recipe 1: Kolaches

The Kolaches have been part of the Christmas breakfast traditions in the Czech Republic for a very long time.

**Duration:** 2 hours 10 minutes

**Makes:** 36

**Ingredient List:**

- ½ of a teaspoons of lemon extract
- 1 cup of shortening
- ½ a cup of brown sugar
- 1 ½ tablespoons of active dry yeast
- 1 ½ teaspoons of salt
- 5 cups of all-purpose flour
- 2 ½ cups of scalded milk
- ½ of a cup of fruit preserves
- 4 egg yolks (beaten)

xxxxxxxxxxxxxxxxxxxxxxxxxxxxxxxxxxxxxxxxxxxxxxxxxxxxxxx

**Methods:**

Get a bowl and cream the shortening with the sugar before stirring in your salt, egg yolks, flavorings, hot milk, and yeast. Let the mix stand for 5 minutes before you add the flour, then beat then and adequately knead it down into a bowl and let the sticky bowl rise for an hour.

Cut the dough into small balls, and then roll them into rounds within your hand before placing them on greased cookie sheets 2 inches apart. Let the dough rise for 15 minutes. Create a depression in the center of each roll, then fill the depression with some fruit preserves. Bake the rolls until they turn brown inside a 450 degree F oven (this should take between 30 to 60 minutes) and cool them on wire racks before serving.

# Recipe 2: Pumpkin with Apricot, Served with Couscous

Lamb couscous is ideal for gatherings with family and friends.

**Duration:** 1 hour

**Makes:** 4

**Ingredient List:**

- ¼ of a cup of San Remo couscous
- 500g of butternut pumpkin (must be peeled and cut into chunks)
- 2 teaspoons of oily spray
- 1 teaspoon of ground pepper (freshly ground)
- 1 juiced lemon
- ¼ of a cup of boiling water
- 1 pack (150g) of dried apricot (cut into pieces)
- 60g of chopped pistachio kennels
- 1 cup of chopped continental parsley
- 1 pack (400g) of lean lamb back-strap
- ½ teaspoons of salt
- ½ a cup of low-fat tzatziki

xxxxxxxxxxxxxxxxxxxxxxxxxxxxxxxxxxxxxxxxxxxxxxxxxxxxx

**Methods:**

Pre-heat the oven to about 430 degrees F, then place the pumpkin inside a baking tray before spraying with oil—Season the with pepper before roasting for about 40 minutes when it should have turned golden. Get a large bowl, and inside, place the couscous, then add some lemon juice inside a cup before topping it up with boiling water to make 1 ½ cups. Stir and cover the ingredients in the cup, let it stand for about 6 minutes, and then fluff it with a fork.

Add the apricots to the couscous and the pistachios, pumpkin, and parsley, then mix properly. Season your lamb with salt and pepper before cooking over high heat for about 5 minutes on each side. Allow the cooked lamb to stand for about 5 minutes before you serve with the couscous and tzatziki.

# Recipe 3: The Wild Rice Soup

If you enjoy the taste of flour in your soup, this could be one of the best choices to consider.

**Makes:** 4

**Duration:** 35 minutes

**Ingredient List:**

- 1/3 cup of butter
- 1 cup of carrots (diced)
- 1 cup of diced celery
- 3 cups of chicken broths
- ½ a cup of flour
- ¼ cup of sliced almonds
- 1 cup of milk
- 2 cups of wild rice soup (cooked)
- 1 cup of diced ham, turkey or chicken
- ½ teaspoons each of salt and pepper

xxxxxxxxxxxxxxxxxxxxxxxxxxxxxxxxxxxxxxxxxxxxxxxxxxxxxxxxx

**Methods:**

Sauté the carrots, onion, and celery inside the butter and in a moderately large pot, then blend in the flour and your chicken broth. Stir the mixture constantly and bring to a boil. Add the ham, chicken, or turkey, and then the wild rice almonds before spicing it with salt and pepper. Heat and blend in the milk before serving.

# Recipe 4: Rye Bread Pudding

Rye bread will always taste great in a pudding any day.

**Makes:** 1-2

**Duration:** 3 hours 20 minutes

**Ingredient List:**

- 1 ½ cups of rye bread crumbs
- ½ cup of sugar
- 4 large eggs
- 1 pinch of cloves
- 1 pinch of allspice
- 1 ½ teaspoons of cinnamon
- 1 rind of half lemon (grated)
- ¼ lbs. of chopped almonds
- 3 teaspoons of whiskey or brandy

xxxxxxxxxxxxxxxxxxxxxxxxxxxxxxxxxxxxxxxxxxxxxxxxxxxxxxxxx

**Methods:**

Dry the rye bread crumbs in the oven for about 5 minutes, get a bowl, and beat the egg yolk with the sugar, then add the cloves, allspices, cinnamon, and rind of lemon before adding the chopped almonds.

Moisten the bread crumbs with the whiskey and then add them to the eggs before adding the stiffly beaten egg whites. Boil the mix inside the mold for about 3 hours before serving.

# Recipe 5: The Czech-Style Zucchini Soup

This is a healthy soup recipe for the precise soup lovers.

**Makes:** 6

**Duration:** 30 minutes

**Ingredient List:**

- 3 tablespoons olive oil
- 1 clove of garlic (chopped)
- 3 medium peeled and cut potatoes
- 1 sliced onion
- 2 stalks of sliced celery
- 2 tablespoons of fresh parsley
- 1 teaspoon of oregano
- R cups of beef stock
- 1 peeled large tomato
- 1 pound of halved zucchini
- 2 teaspoons of salt
- 6 teaspoons of grated parmesan cheese

xxxxxxxxxxxxxxxxxxxxxxxxxxxxxxxxxxxxxxxxxxxxxxxxxxxxxxxx

**Methods:**

Get a large saucepan and then heat the olive oil with the garlic. Discard the garlic once it runs brown. Add the potato and cook for about 5 minutes until they become coated. Add the celery, parsley, onion, and oregano and cook further until the onion becomes soft. Add the stock, salt, tomato, and bring the mix to boil.

Reduce the heat and simmer until the zucchini is tender, then pour the soups into the bowls and sprinkle pepper and parmesan cheese and serve.

# Recipe 6: The Hungarian Poppy Seed Filling

This is a special European filling that is popular in the Czech and the entire mid-European region.

**Duration:** 60 minutes

**Makes:** 16

**Ingredient List:**

- ¾ of a cup of brown sugar
- ½ lb. of poppy seeds
- 1 cup of skimmed milk
- 1 teaspoon of salt
- ¼ of a cup of margarine
- 2 beaten large eggs

xxxxxxxxxxxxxxxxxxxxxxxxxxxxxxxxxxxxxxxxxxxxxxxxxxxxxxxxx

**Methods:**

Get a coffee grinder or mill, and inside, grind the poppy seeds. Get a large bowl, and inside, combine the milk with the margarine and sugar, then pour inside a saucepan. Cook the mix on low heat and occasionally stir until all the sugar has dissolved. Gently pour half of the hot milk into the beaten eggs and whisk continuously. Take the egg and milk mixture back to the saucepan and continue cooking and stirring until the mix starts thickening and coating the back of your metal spoon.

Add the ground poppy seed to your mix and stir very well to blend in. Remove the cooked mix from heat and cool for about 3 minutes before using. You can store this mix inside the refrigerator for up to 5 days.

# Recipe 7: The Carla's Turkey Meatloaf Recipe

This recipe is complemented with several herbal ingredients. Hence it can be regarded as an ideal medicinal meatloaf.

**Makes:** 8

**Duration:** 2 hours 15 minutes

**Ingredient List:**

- 2 lbs. of ground turkey
- 2 tablespoons of hot ketchup
- 1 tablespoon of salt
- 1 finely chopped celery
- 1 teaspoon of thyme
- 1 tablespoon of chopped parsley
- 1 tablespoon of Worcestershire sauce
- 1 medium-sized chopped onion
- ½ teaspoons of pepper
- 1 teaspoon of rosemary
- 1 teaspoon of basil
- ½ cup of oatmeal

xxxxxxxxxxxxxxxxxxxxxxxxxxxxxxxxxxxxxxxxxxxxxxxxxxxxxx

**Methods:**

Mix all the ingredients inside a bowl and form it into a loaf. Place the mix inside a non-stick loaf pan, bake for about 350 degrees F for about 2 hours, and serve immediately.

# Recipe 8: Roast Pork, The National Dish

The delicious Roasted pork will definitely make your day because it contains lots of herbs and veggies.

**Duration:** 3 hours

**Makes:** 2-3

**Ingredient List:**

- 1 tablespoon of vegetable oil
- 1 tablespoon of prepared mustard
- 2 tablespoons of Caraway seeds
- 1 tablespoon of garlic powder
- 1 tablespoon of salt
- 1 teaspoon of black pepper (ground)
- 2 lbs. of pork roast
- 1 medium of chopped onion,
- ½ a cup of water
- 1 tablespoon of corn starch
- 2 tablespoons of butter

xxxxxxxxxxxxxxxxxxxxxxxxxxxxxxxxxxxxxxxxxxxxxxxxxxxxx

**Methods:**

Get a large bowl, and inside, mix the mustard with the vegetable oil, with mustard, pepper, salt, garlic powder, ad caraway seeds, then rub the mix on the pork before you let it sit for about 40 minutes. Pre-heat the oven to about 325 degrees F, then put the onions inside a roasting pan before pouring the water. Put your pork roast on top of the onion inside the pan before covering the pan with foil. You may add some garlic cloves before baking in the oven, but make sure you turn the meat while baking (the baking should last for about 1 ½ hours).

Save the juices from the pan and add your corn starch and butter before simmering until the mi thickens. Simply pour the corn starch mix on the pork and dumplings before serving.

# Recipe 9: The Simple Creamy and Delicious Broccoli Soup

This should be your favorite broccoli recipe that is lighter and easier to prepare.

**Makes:** 8

**Duration:** 25 minutes

**Ingredient List:**

- Fresh broccoli florets 9 (3 bags)
- A large chopped onion
- A clove of minced garlic
- 2 quarts of chicken broth
- 1 cup of milk or cream
- ½ teaspoons each of pepper and salt
- ¼ cup of chopped dill or basil
- Optional 2 cups of tiny pasta

xxxxxxxxxxxxxxxxxxxxxxxxxxxxxxxxxxxxxxxxxxxxxxxxxxxxxxxx

**Methods:**

Rinse the florets of broccoli and then cover them with water. Add the onion and cook until broccoli becomes tender. Drain and keep the cooking water, and then move the florets and onion mix into a large cooking pot before adding sufficient stock to cover the mixture.

With the aid of the hand blender, chop the broccoli but make sure you don't puree. Heat the mix and season with pepper and salt. Add the milk or cream, then add pasta if you need to thicken the mixture further. Garnish the bowls for soup with some sour cream or sprinkle some fresh herbs. Serve immediately with crackers.

# Recipe 10: The Easy Czechoslovakia Vegetable Soup Recipe

This is a hearty winter squash soup you can enjoy alone or with friends and family

**Makes:** 4

**Duration:** 35 minutes

**Ingredient List:**

- 2lbs whole pumpkin
- 1 chopped onion
- 2 cups of chicken or vegetable stock
- 1 tablespoon of mild powder (chili)
- 1 cup of cooked white beans
- 1 cup of frozen beans (lima)
- 1 cup of cooked brown rice
- 1 cup of fresh or frozen corn kernels
- ½ cup of chopped red bell peppers
- ½ teaspoons each of salt and pepper

xxxxxxxxxxxxxxxxxxxxxxxxxxxxxxxxxxxxxxxxxxxxxxxxxxxxxxxxx

**Methods:**

Prepare the pumpkin by puncturing it in several places with a knife or fork, then place it in the microwave for about 5 minutes until it is soft enough. Cut the pumpkin in half and cool down before scrapping the seeds. Boil the quarter of a cup of stock and add your onions and cook further for about 10 minutes.

Stir in the remainder of the stock, white beans, and seasonings. Simmer the soup gently until your pumpkin is ready. Scoop the pumpkin's flesh inside the soup, add your lima beans, grains, and corn, and let the mix simmer until the rice grains and beans are soft. Serve immediately.

# Recipe 11: The Czech Cabbage Dish

This cabbage dish is one of the most popular dishes at family gatherings and friends' reunions in the Czech republic.

**Duration:** 30 minutes

**Makes:** 10

**Ingredient List:**

- 1 shredded head of large cabbage
- ¼ of chopped green bell pepper
- ¼ of a pound of chopped bacon
- 3 tablespoons of white vinegar
- 1 tablespoon of vegetable oil
- ½ teaspoons of salt
- 1 small chopped onion
- 1 teaspoon of black pepper (ground)
- 1 stalk of chopped celery

xxxxxxxxxxxxxxxxxxxxxxxxxxxxxxxxxxxxxxxxxxxxxxxxxxxxxxx

**Methods:**

Get slightly salted water inside a pot to boil, then Blanche the cabbage briefly in the boiling water and remove after 2 minutes to drain immediately.

Get a large skillet, and inside brown the bacon over medium heat until it turns opaque, then remove the bacon and drain on a paper towel. Remove the bacon grease from the skillet (leave 1 tablespoon), then add the vegetable oil before eating the cabbage over medium heat. Add the bell pepper, celery, and onion, and then sauté until it becomes crispy. Get a new and clean large bowl, and inside mix the prepared cabbage with the bacon and sautéed vegetable mix. Add the vinegar, salt, pepper and mix appropriately before chilling or serving warm.

# Recipe 12: The Czech Grandma's Meatloaf

This is a typical meatloaf recipe loved by the grandmas, and it will definitely make your day.

**Makes:** 8

**Duration:** 1 hour 15 minutes

**Ingredient List:**

- 1 large beaten egg
- ¼ of a cup of dry bread crumbs
- 3 slices of bacon (cut into ¼" pieces)
- 1 large chopped onion
- 2 oz. of cubed cheddar
- ½ teaspoons of salt
- ½ teaspoons of pepper
- 1 lean beef (ground)
- ½ lbs. of Pork sausage

xxxxxxxxxxxxxxxxxxxxxxxxxxxxxxxxxxxxxxxxxxxxxxxxxxxxxx

**Methods:**

Pre-heat the oven to about 450 degrees F, form the mix into a loaf, and then bake for about 45 minutes. Cool for few minutes and serve immediately.

# Recipe 13: The Czech Raisins with Bread Pudding

Raisins with sweet milk alongside bread crumbs can produce one of the best puddings you can ever ask for.

**Makes:** 2-3

**Duration:** 1 hour 20 minutes

**Ingredient List:**

- 2 slices (bread crumbs)
- A pint of sweet milk
- 2 eggs
- 1 Grated lemon juice
- 2 teaspoons of raisins
- 3 teaspoons of sugar
- 2 tablespoons of jelly

xxxxxxxxxxxxxxxxxxxxxxxxxxxxxxxxxxxxxxxxxxxxxxxxxxx

**Methods:**

Soak the bread slices in the sweet milk for about 30 minutes, then get a bowl, and inside, separate the egg yolk from the whites, keep the egg white somewhere until they are needed. Beat the egg yolk inside the sugar and add the grated lemon peel before stirring the mix of the bread crumbs.

Put some raisins, add the final mix into a greased pudding dish, and bake for about half an hour in the 350 degrees F oven. Return to the egg white and beat it until it becomes stiff froth, add 2 teaspoons of sugar, spread it over the pudding, return the pudding to the oven, and bake until it turns brown. Remove from oven and spread jelly sauce on it.

# Recipe 14: The Czechoslovakia Black Bread

# Pudding

The rye bread is sometimes referred to as black bread, and it helps create one of the best delicious family puddings.

**Makes:** 2-3 slices of pudding (1 large pudding)

**Duration:** 1 hour 20 minutes

**Ingredient List:**

- 3 egg yolk
- ½ cup of sugar
- 1 pinch of cloves
- 1 cup of stale rye bread crumbs
- 1 teaspoon of Cinnamon
- 1 pinch allspice
- 3 egg whites
- 1 cup of claret or white wine

xxxxxxxxxxxxxxxxxxxxxxxxxxxxxxxxxxxxxxxxxxxxxxxxxxxxxxxxx

**Methods:**

Beat the egg yolk with the sugar and the cinnamon. Before adding the cloves and rye bread, mix very well, and add the egg whites before mixing again. Bake slowly in the oven for about 1 hour, then add the white or claret wine, some 30 minutes before serving the pudding.

# Recipe 15: The Czechoslovakian Cookies

These are spicy and crunchy bar cookies, common in Czechoslovakia cities

**Duration:** 2 hours

**Makes:** 12

**Ingredient List:**

- ¼ of a teaspoons of ground allspice
- 1 cup of butter
- 1 cup of brown sugar
- 2 cups of all-purpose flour
- 1 cup of pelicans (chopped)
- 2 large egg yolks
- 1 teaspoon of vanilla extract
- ½ a cup of strawberry jam
- 1/8 teaspoons of ground cardamom.

xxxxxxxxxxxxxxxxxxxxxxxxxxxxxxxxxxxxxxxxxxxxxxxxxxxxxxxx

**Methods:**

Pre-heat the oven to about 330 degrees F and grease a single 8-inch sq. baking dish. Cream your butter until it becomes soft and fluffy, then add the sugar, gradually until the mix becomes light and fluffy. Beat in your egg yolk. Sift in the cardamom, flour, and allspice together, then slowly mix it into your butter mixture before stirring to combine perfectly. Stir in your chopped pecans likewise.

Spoon half of your prepared dough into the prepared pan and spread it evenly. Top it up with the strawberry jam before covering it with the remaining dough. Bake the dough for 1 hour until it becomes light brown, then cut into 1 ½ inch squares before serving.

# Recipe 16: The Bramboracky (Czech Savory Potato Recipe)

This is a traditional Czech pan-fried potato that is usually served with different kinds of drinks.

**Duration:** 1 hour

**Makes:** 3

**Ingredient List:**

- 4 medium to large potatoes
- 2 large eggs
- 3 cloves of crushed garlic
- 1 tablespoon of milk
- ½ teaspoons of salt
- ½ teaspoons of pepper
- 3 tablespoons of all-purpose flour
- 1 pinch of dried marjoram (optional)
- 2 teaspoons of oil
- 2 teaspoons of caraway seeds (optional)

xxxxxxxxxxxxxxxxxxxxxxxxxxxxxxxxxxxxxxxxxxxxxxxxxxxxxxxxxx

**Methods:**

Peel the potatoes and grate them coarsely (make sure you squeeze out as much liquid as you can), put the shredded potato inside a bowl, and stir in your crushed garlic pepper, marjoram, salt, and caraway seeds. Get a new bowl, and inside, beat the egg inside alongside the milk, then add the egg mix to the potatoes before stirring well to combine. Mix in the flour gradually to form a thick but slurry batter.

Get a skillet and heat oil over medium heat (make sure the oil is about ¼ inch deep), then spoon about a quarter of a cup of the batter into the oil before flattening the batter slightly. Fry your pancake until it becomes golden brown. You may taste a pancake before adjusting the seasoning. Repeat the frying with the remaining batter.

# Recipe 17: The Listy L Recipe

Often pronounced as "Listy Tay," this is one of the most delicious Czech grandmother recipes.

**Duration:** 1 hour

**Makes:** 24 minutes

**Ingredient List:**

- 3 large egg yolks
- 1 cup of egg white
- 2 teaspoons of light whipping cream
- 1 ½ cups of all-purpose flour
- ¼ of a teaspoon of salt
- 2 tablespoons of confectioners' sugar
- 2 tablespoons of brown sugar
- 1 cup of vegetable oil

xxxxxxxxxxxxxxxxxxxxxxxxxxxxxxxxxxxxxxxxxxxxxxxxxxxxxxx

**Methods:**

Get a bowl and inside mix the egg yolks, salt, sugar, egg white, and cream and gradually stir in the flour until a dough that is stiff enough to be rolled is formed. Roll out a paper-thin and cut into triangles, then slit each twist's mid region to make it look more appealing.

Add some oil into the pot to cover your cookies, then heat the oil until it can fry some tiny amount of dough. Deep-fry each of the cookies inside the hot oil until they turn light brown, remove the cookies before draining them inside paper towels, sprinkle the confectioner's sugar before serving.

# Recipe 18: The Traditional Czech Fiery Couscous

This couscous recipe comes with many healthy components that will increase your metabolism. Hence it is perfect for weight watchers.

**Duration:** 30 minutes

**Makes:** 4

**Ingredient List:**

- 1 cup of couscous (San Remo)
- ½ a cup of ground Caraway seeds
- 1 tablespoon of olive oil
- 2 cloves of crushed garlic
- ½ a teaspoons of harissa
- 1 teaspoon of paprika (sweet)
- 1 teaspoon of ground caraway
- 1 (50g) sachet of tomato paste
- 1 cup of water
- 1 cup (450g) of drained chickpeas
- 100g of reduced-fat crumbled Feta

xxxxxxxxxxxxxxxxxxxxxxxxxxxxxxxxxxxxxxxxxxxxxxxxxxxxxxxx

**Methods:**

Get a saucepan, and inside, heat the oil with the harissa and garlic for about 2 minutes when it becomes fragrant. Add the tomato paste and the water before bringing to a boil. Remove from the heat before stirring in the couscous, then cover and let it stand for about 5 minutes. Fluff the mix with a fork and allow it to cool. Stir it in the chickpeas before sprinkling the feta, then serve immediately.

# Recipe 19: The Czech Caraway-Rye Bread

Caraway seeds are popular in the Czech Republic, and they can be prepared for different meals.

**Duration:** 45 minutes

**Makes:** 20

**Ingredient List:**

- 2 packages of active dry yeast
- 1 tablespoon of vegetable oil
- 2 cups of warm water (divided)
- 2 teaspoons of salt
- ¼ of a cup of packed brown sugar
- 2 ½ cups of rye flour
- 1 tablespoon of caraway seed
- 2 ¾ cups of all-purpose flour (divided)

xxxxxxxxxxxxxxxxxxxxxxxxxxxxxxxxxxxxxxxxxxxxxxxxxxxxxx

**Methods:**

Get a large mixing bowl and dissolve the yeast inside half a cup of warm water. Add the caraway, brown sugar, oil, salt as well as the remaining water. Mix properly before stirring in the rye flour plus the all-purpose flour. Beat the dough until very smooth.

Add the remaining all-purpose flour to create a soft dough, then turn it onto the floured surface before kneading until it becomes smooth and elastic (this should take 8 minutes). Place the bowl inside a greased bowl before turning it into the greased top, then cover it and let it stay in a warm place until it swells and double in size (this should take 1 hour). Punch the dough down, and then divide it into half before shaping each half into balls.

Place the balls inside 8-inch greased round cake pans before flattening the balls into 6-inch diameter. Cover the dough and let it rise until it becomes doubled in size (this should take 30 minutes). Bake the dough for 30 minutes in the oven, at 375 degrees F, when it turns golden brown.

# Author's Afterthoughts

I can't appreciate you enough for spending your precious time reading my book. If there is anything that gladdens an author's heart, it is that his or her work be read. And I am extremely joyous that my labor and the hours put into making this publication a reality didn't go to waste.

Another thing that gladdens an author's heart is feedback because every comment from the good people who read one's book matters a great deal in helping you become better at what you do.

This is why I wouldn't shy away from reading your thoughts and comments about what you have read in this publication.

Do you think it is good enough? Do you think it could be better?

Please keep the feedback coming in, I won't hesitate to read any of them!!!

*Thanks!*

*Layla Tacy*

# Biography

Climbing up the ladder from a young girl who loved to experiment with food items in her mother's cottage kitchen at the tender age of 7, to changing cooking from what it was to what it should be; Layla has more than made a name for herself, but she has created a dynasty for herself in the cooking world.

With more than twenty-five years in the culinary world, Layla has grown to be an authority with her influence spreading all over different high-class hotels and restaurants in and around Kansas City, such as Hilton President Kansas City, The Fountaine hotel, and Embassy Suites.

After working as a chef in different establishments, Layla moved on to become a chef-trainer to several up-and-coming chefs. Currently, she has graduated more than 200 trainees at her Chef School and presently has about 150 graduates in her school.

Printed in Great Britain
by Amazon